CH

NIGHT

RHONA PIPE

ILLUSTRATIONS BY MAGGIE DOWNER

It all began when an angel
came to see Mary. She was
a country girl from the village
of Nazareth up in the hills.
She was engaged to be married
and her mind was full of
plans for her wedding, not angels.

"Hello," the angel said. "God has
made you happy and He is
with you."

It was strange and frightening.
What did the angel mean?

"Don't be afraid," the angel said, "You will have a baby son. He'll be a great king — forever."

"But I'm not married yet," Mary said.

"Your baby will be God's Son," the angel replied. "Everything is possible with God."

"I'll do whatever God wishes," Mary said. "I'm God's servant."

Soon everyone in Nazareth knew
that Mary was expecting a baby.

"She ought to be
ashamed," people muttered.

Mary was engaged to
a carpenter called Joseph.
He was very upset.
"That wild story
about an angel can't
be true, can it?" he
said to himself, "How
can I marry Mary
now? It's all over."

But God was looking after Mary.
He sent an angel to speak
to Joseph. The angel came in
the night, when Joseph was asleep.

"Don't be afraid to marry
Mary," the angel said. "Her baby
is God's Son. You must call
Him Jesus."

The word "Jesus" means "God
saves."

As soon as Joseph woke up
he rushed to see Mary. They
got married right away.

Mary and Joseph began
to get everything
ready for the baby.
Then another
surprising thing
happened.

Roman soldiers came riding into
town with orders from the Emperor.
ATTENTION
the orders said.
URGENT
You all have to go back
to your hometowns and put
your names on a list.

Bethlehem was Joseph's
town. The journey was long
and slow. Mary's back ached.

"Sorry," the innkeeper said when
they arrived. "No room. We're full."

The innkeeper looked thoughtfully at Mary. "Well," he said, "you might just be able to squeeze into the stable."

That night Jesus was born.

Mary wrapped Him in strips of cloth, as mothers did in those days. His cradle was back in Nazareth, so Mary put Jesus down to sleep in the manger, where the cows and donkeys usually ate their hay.

It was quiet in the stable.

That night, in the fields outside Bethlehem, a group of shepherds got the biggest surprise of their lives. They kept telling their story to anyone who would listen.

"There we were, keeping an eye on our sheep, minding our own business," they said, "when there was a blinding light and an angel. 'Don't be scared,' he said 'it's good news.'"

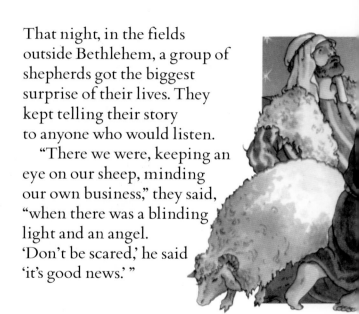

The shepherds said, "The angel told
us about our Saviour being born here
in Bethlehem. And no sooner had
he finished than the music began.
Singing, like you've never heard before.
There were crowds of them — angels —
all praising God. Then they
were gone, leaving us standing there
in the dark with our mouths hanging
open. 'What are we waiting for?'
we said. 'Come on. Let's go.' "

"Sure enough, there was the baby,"
the shepherds said to everyone they met.

That first Christmas night a new star shone in the sky.

"How remarkable!" said some wise men, far away in the east.

"What does it mean?"

They studied their books.

"A king has been born. Who is he?" They studied some more.

"The Jews are waiting for a king. We must go at once to the royal palace in Jerusalem," the wise men said, "and worship a king who is greeted by a star."

In Jerusalem King Herod was definitely
not happy. "I'm the only king
around here," he said to himself,
"and it's going to stay that way."

He summoned his counsellors and
courtiers, his priests and politicians.

"What's going on?" he demanded.
"A king," they said. "In Bethlehem."
"We'll see about that," Herod said.
He met the wise men, secretly.
"Tell me when you find him," he
murmured, "so I may worship him, too."

Outside Jerusalem, they saw the star.

The wise men bowed before the baby, their eyes full of wonder.

They gave their presents — gold, sweet-smelling frankincense and myrrh.

But they would not stop. "You're in danger," they said. "An angel has warned us not to go back to Jerusalem. We will go home another way so that Herod will not know where to find you."

They left at once, happy because God was taking care of His Son.